T0380961

Nana's Bits & Pieces

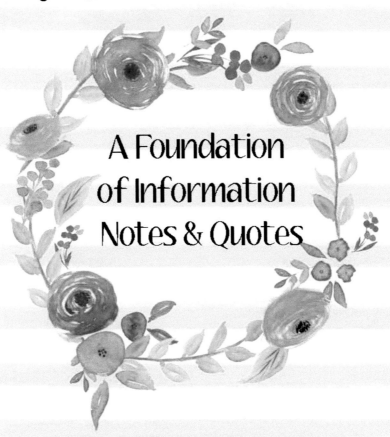

A Foundation
of Information
Notes & Quotes

To order additional copies of this book, contact:
Xlibris
1-888-795-4274
www.Xlibris.com
Orders@Xlibris.com

Nana's Bits & Pieces

A Foundation
of Information
Notes & Quotes

Written By:
Kate Pecoraro
♡ 2017

Nana's Bits & Pieces

A Foundation of Informational
Notes and Quotes

Written With Love By: Kate Pecoraro

2017

Table of Contents

Letter From The Heart

To my precious children, their spouses, children, grandchildren and great grandchildren

I hope that life will be your treasure box filled with laugher, adventure, magic, and love; the best jewel of all.

Each time you succeed, no matter how tiny success, stop for a minute and listen for a cheer. That's me. No matter where you are or where I am, I'm cheering for you. I am thankful for nights that turn into mornings, friends that turned into family, and dreams that turned into reality.

May God bless my family and friends, especially those who need a miracle today. Strengthen those who are weak and make them strong. But most of all, thank you for the gift of TODAY!

A Fountain of Information
Notes & Quotes

As I start each day with a Prayer,

I start this book with one too!

"I am a mother and grandmother Dear Lord,"

I ask nothing from you for me.

I pray only that in your mercy you would grant my children and grandchildren their needs.

May their lives be long and healthy. May they achieve all their dreams.

May they always live in a world that is free.

May they be who they are born to be; and may they know to their and my last days they were deeply love by me.

Things Learned and Lived

I've lived and learned many things in my life and I'd love to share some of the things that were and are important to me:

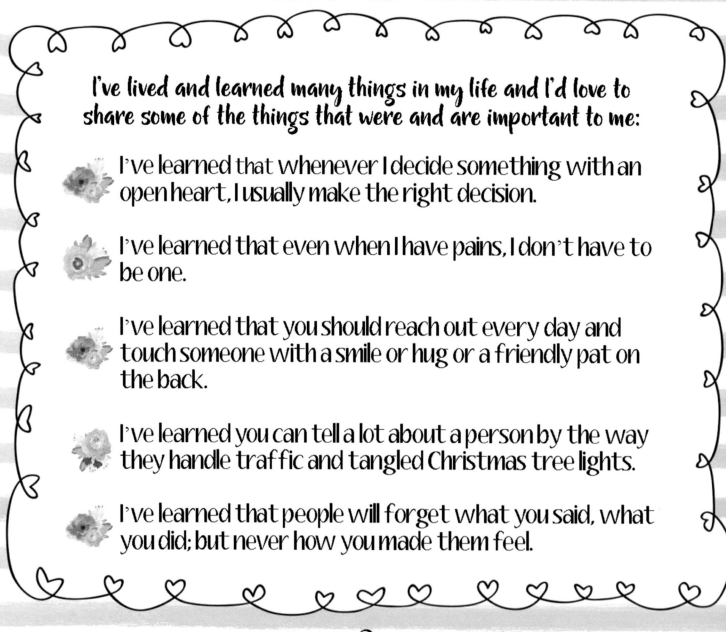

I've learned that whenever I decide something with an open heart, I usually make the right decision.

I've learned that even when I have pains, I don't have to be one.

I've learned that you should reach out every day and touch someone with a smile or hug or a friendly pat on the back.

I've learned you can tell a lot about a person by the way they handle traffic and tangled Christmas tree lights.

I've learned that people will forget what you said, what you did; but never how you made them feel.

I've learned when I hear the song "Let It Be" it can lift my spirits.

I've learned that you need to be able to both pitch and catch.

I've learned the greater a person's sense of guilt, the greater the need to blame someone else.

I've learned that you love your children more than anything in the world; but the people in the restaurant, movie theatre, and grocery store don't, so beware of how they are behaving.

I've learned that I never stop learning.

Seek solutions to problems, instead of complaining which leads no where. Do not engage in negative self talk. Mistakes are made, accept them and move on. Regret is harmful and a constant reminder of past decisions. Can be a reason for stress and depression

Now To The Subject of Romance

Romance makes you feel special, it makes every woman beautiful, and every man a prince. With Romance in your heart, you are both King & Queen because your heart is treasured. You do things, happy things because you love that person. You selfishly give because it makes you happy.

LOVE

When you love, love in both Words and Deeds.
You only have what you can give. Love and Magic have a great deal in common. They enrich the soul and delight the heart. They both take unrelenting time and practice. The starting point of all achievement is desire. Weak desire brings weak results. A small amount of fire makes a small amount of heat. In life, you will realize that there is a role for everyone you meet. Some will test you, some will use you, some will love you, and some will teach you. But, the ones that are important are the ones who bring out the best in you. They're the rare and amazing people who will remind you why all relationships are worth it.

Happiness

"What Makes Me Happy" is an overused statement.

"Most people have a wrong idea of what constitutes true happiness. It is not attained through self-gratification, but fidelity to a worthy purpose." ♡ Helen Keller

Pleasure is of the body; joy is of the mind. Steak gives you pleasure; but not even the most avid steak lover would say it makes them joyful. You can quickly become tired of pleasures; but you can never tire of joys. Remember always; there's not so much as a port in a storm; but a hand to hold as the storm passes. Always pray to have eyes that see the best, a heart that forgives the worst, a mind that forgets the bad, and a soul that never loses faith. You cannot talk defeat and expect to have a victory. You can't talk lack and expect an abundance. You've got to send your thoughts and words in the direction you want your life to go.

"Stupidity is one of the two things we must clearly see in retrospect; the other is missed chances."

Stress

Next time you're stressed
take a step back, inhale and laugh.

Remember who you are and why you are here. Be strong, love yourself, and always keep moving forward. Someday, everything will make perfect sense. So, for now, laugh at the confusion, smile through the tears and keep reminding yourself that everything happens for a reason.

"Let It Be", my favorite Beatles song.

"What lies behind us and what lies before us are tiny matters compared to what lies within us."

Ralph W. Emerson

Turn your back on the cloudy days of the past and look towards the rainbows that promise a beautiful future.

Rules for a Healthy Relationship

1. Love with an open heart! Forgive without a reason.
2. Pray.
3. Be strong and tender at the same time.
4. Give flowers for no reason.
5. Make your partner feel valued.
6. Better to be kind than right.
7. You set the tone for a sexual relationship. Don't take something away you can't give back.
8. Laugh, have a sense of humor.
9. Know what the dishwasher, oven, vacuum cleaner, washing machines are and use them.
10. Call your mother & grandmother because we will be there for you always.

Drama

There comes a time in life when you walk away from the drama and the people who create it. Surround yourself with people who make you **laugh** and have no agenda but what's best for you. Love the people who treat you right. Pray for the ones who don't. Life is too short to be anything but happy. Falling down is part of life, how you get up is part of living. When I reflect on my life I realize that every time I thought I was rejected from something good, I was actually being redirected to something better.

LET'S TALK MARRIAGE

Marriage is not about happiness. It's not a magic box where we can pull our happiness. It's a commitment for life and an opportunity to grow together. It's a connection and a determination to care for your partner. It is not passive, nor is it a victim. Your happiness lies in the happiness of others. Give out happiness and you will find yours. Prove the things you claim and always reveal the real you. Teamwork is key. Savor life's joys. Enjoy one day at a time. Cultivate optimism and avoid comparisons. Life is made up of moments filled with joy, some anger and some sadness. The hope is at the end of the day, there will be balance, light/dark, sorrow/gladness.

Good Relationships

NEVER   pulls apart a family.

NEVER   asks anyone to give up their passions.

NEVER   wants to be taken care of; but appreciates being cared for.

NEVER   changes flaws, annoying habits, funny traits, but finds them endearing.

NEVER   ignores, controls, or jumps to conclusions.

NEVER   demands all their time.

Finances (NOT MY STRONG SUIT)

I can say from experience, be honest, plan and share. A budget is always good and communication is key. Never let what you want make you forget what you have. It's in the spending of yourselves that you can become rich.

Hurt Feelings

Hurt people, hurt people; that's how pain gets passed on. Meet anger with sympathy, contempt with compassion, and cruelty with kindness. "Surrender to what is, let go of what was, and have faith in what will be." Sometimes the best thing you can do is not think, not wonder, not imagine, not obsess, just breath and have faith.

Acceptance

Nothing, absolutely nothing, happens by mistake. Until I accept myself, my situation, I cannot be happy. You need to concentrate, not so much as what happens in the world, as what needs to change in my attitude. The less you respond to negativity the more peaceful you'll become. Pretty is what you are. Beauty is what you do with it.

Technology

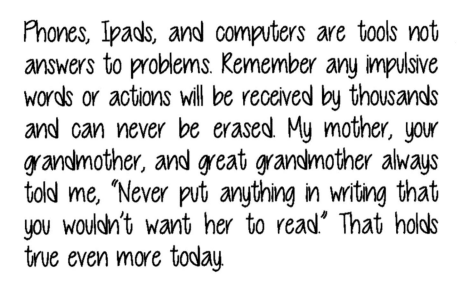

Phones, Ipads, and computers are tools not answers to problems. Remember any impulsive words or actions will be received by thousands and can never be erased. My mother, your grandmother, and great grandmother always told me, "Never put anything in writing that you wouldn't want her to read." That holds true even more today.

Goals

Commit to goals. Most people fall short of goals because they lack commitment. Make short term and long term goals. Share them or write them down. Being accountable helps with success. Challenge yourself daily. ✷ Please, above all else, do not feel entitled. You work, you earn. You give, you get. You love and you are loved. The key to winning is to find no emotion in losing. ✷ Aim high and fight for what you believe. ✷ Let go of what's gone and be grateful for what remains. ✷ Understand fact and opinion, and understand the difference. ✷ Take chances. Remember how foolish it was to worry about re-arranging the pictures and table settings on the "Titanic". ✷ Be thankful for what gifts you have. ✷ Grow a backbone and a wishbone, and know the difference. Wishes and dreams do come true. And a backbone will get you up and going. ♡♡♡You are important and you are needed. Don't wait for someday. Someday is now and that someone is you.

Wisdom

In troubling times such as now, with politics, and countries in turmoil, disrespect is everywhere. Remember your opinions are yours and others who may not agree with you are not to be criticized. They are also entitled to their opinions. Listen to what others say and debate with an open heart. Honesty and violence don't co-exist. Your beliefs, your rights or wrongs are who you are. Insults and hateful words and deeds can never be taken away. Everyone has their reasons, their pains and their passions. We are here equally and hopefully for the common good.

I value the written and the spoken word. Use them with care and truth. Pray as if ALL things depend on God, and work as if ALL things depend on you!!

My Gifts to You

To Those Who Are Angry	♡ Forgiveness
To A Friend	♡ Your Heart
To A Child	♡ Good Example
To An Opponent	♡ Tolerance
To A Customer	♡ Service
To All	♡ Be Clear
To Yourself	♡ Respect

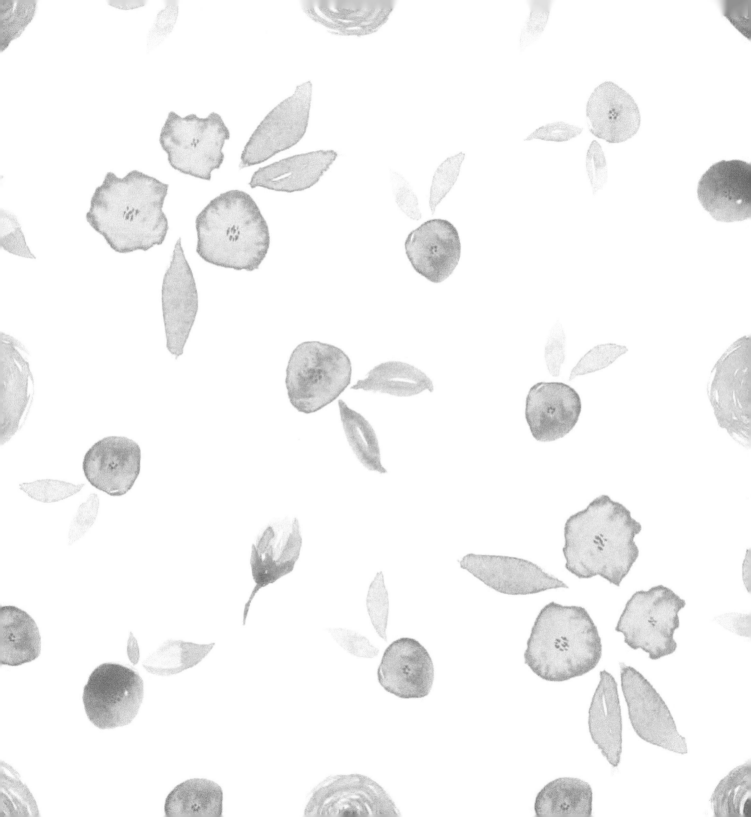

Written By:
Kate Pecoraro
♡ 2017

Printed in the United States
By Bookmasters